COME AND SHOW ME ANOTHER CITY WITH LIFTED HEAD SINGING
SO PROUD TO BE ALIVE AND COARSE AND STRONG AND CUNNING.

CARL SANDBURG

From his poem "Chicago," in the *Chicago Poems*. Born in Galesburg, Illinois, in 1878, Carl Sandburg moved to Chicago as an adult. Known primarily for his often vernacular, free-verse poetry, he won the Pulitzer Prize for his six-volume biography of Abraham Lincoln.

(Overleaf, pages 2-3) Federal Reserve Bank of Chicago. (Overleaf, pages 4-5) Chicago Skyline. (Overleaf, pages 6-7) Chicago Mercantile Exchange. (Overleaf, pages 8-9) Buckingham Fountain, Grant Park. (Overleaf, pages 10-11) Boat basin, Chicago Harbor. (Above) Arch Detail, Goodman Theater Garden.

Designed by Marilyn F. Appleby.
Edited by Kathleen D. Valenzi, Carlotta M. Eike,
Ross A. Howell Jr., and Mary S. Coryell.
Photographs copyright ©1988 by Robert Llewellyn. All rights reserved.
Introduction copyright ©1988 by Steve Allen. All rights reserved.
This book, or any portions thereof, may not be reproduced
or transmitted in any form or by any means, electronic or mechanical, including photocopying,
recording, or by any information storage and retrieval system, without permission
in writing from the publisher.
Photographs may not be reproduced without permission of Robert Llewellyn.
Introduction may not be reproduced without permission of Steve Allen.
Library of Congress Catalog Card Number 88-80086
ISBN 0-943231-05-1
Printed and bound in Hong Kong by Everbest Printing Co., Ltd.,
for Four Colour Imports, Ltd., Louisville, Kentucky.
Published by Howell Press, Inc., 2000 Holiday Drive,
Charlottesville, Virginia 22901. Telephone (804) 977-4006.
First Edition

HOWELL PRESS

CHICAGO

PHOTOGRAPHY BY ROBERT LLEWELLYN

INTRODUCTION BY STEVE ALLEN

GROWING UP IN CHICAGO

by Steve Allen

■

Chicago is as close to a hometown as I have. While I was born in New York City, I spent more of my early years in Chicago than in any other place. A good part of that time was spent in Chicago's Englewood and Hyde Park districts, and my chief hangout was the corner of 54th and Woodlawn.

I attended mostly parochial schools. The three Chicago high schools in which I was enrolled were Mt. Carmel, Hirsh, and Hyde Park. Sometimes I would ditch classes in order to go, not to a pool hall, but to the Museum of Science and Industry or to a library, "searching for the wisdom of the ages," as I wrote in a poem "Chicago: Adolescence." I seem to profit more from self-education than from the formal kind.

I think when you're 10 years old, you could be growing up inside the Vatican, and you wouldn't recognize the location's cultural significance. You just wonder where the next ice cream bar is coming from or what time the other kids will come back with a ball and bat so you can play.

It was only as an adult that I perceived Chicago's history and its cultural importance. For example, I was totally unaware, even as a teen-ager living in the south side, of the contribution Frank Lloyd Wright made to that area and to architecture in general. There was one house I passed almost daily, and only about 30 years later did I realize that it had been designed and constructed according to Mr. Wright's specifications.

I enjoyed Chicago, Lake Michigan, the museums, and the libraries. When I was quite young—five or six years old—an uncle, Steve Donahue, would take me to the Lincoln Park Zoo from time to time or to the circus when it was in town. Once or twice we went to a baseball game.

Chicago, as does that part of the temporal zone around the planet, has its weather extremes—very hot in the summer, bitterly cold in the winter. I recall one year when it was about 20 degrees below zero for a couple of days. From having to move about in that weather, I learned that cold beyond a certain point is experienced as a kind of pain. The pain was so severe that you could not walk more than a block at a time. On my way home from school, I would move from the school to a drug store, from the drug

(Facing) Chicago River.

store to a candy store, from the candy store to a cigar stand, and so on. I had to keep getting off the street every few minutes in order to become human again before I could dash out to make another block's progress.

I have a memory of a strikingly beautiful sight one Chicago winter. It was the year my mother and I lived in the near north side, and I would sometimes walk across one of the bridges to get a streetcar for the south side to visit friends. There had been a heavy snowfall during the previous night, and the bridge I intended to cross was covered with fresh snow, untouched by human feet. I stood facing the structure, marvelling at the snow's beauty, when a boat slowly came down the river. The bridge was raised in the middle to allow the boat to pass. As the angle of the rising bridge halves became increasingly steep, there came a point when all the snow tumbled down in two symmetrical avalanches. I've never forgotten that sight.

I spent a lot of time on Lake Michigan as a child, particularly when I was living in the Hyde Park neighborhood. The lake was a godsend. Those were the days before air conditioning, and Chicago summers were not much fun, as far as the climate was concerned. The lake kept you in your right mind during the heat of the summer months.

There was a tunnel in Jackson Park that I used to frequent with my friend Bob Petrolli. Tunnels are interesting acoustically, and at the time, I was teach-

ing myself to play an old, beat-up trumpet that I'd bought at a pawnshop for ten dollars. I would play the horn inside the tunnel, and Bob and I would listen to the amplified sound coming back at us. The noise must have deafened anyone who came walking through while we were there.

Bob and I also used to take the trumpet out on the rowboats in Jackson Park in the evening. Unaided by other accompaniment, the instrument doesn't sound too marvelous out over water, but it was fun to do it. I wrote about the experience in a poem called "June Night."

We used to go out in the rowboats
Laughing in the summer night,
Put trumpets to our unsure lips
And blow wild cracking notes across the black lagoon.

We used to listen to them echo
From the walls of the museum
Under the cool Chicago stars.
We would laugh the rough animal cackle
While lovers whispered curses to the water.

Once, on a dark, moonless night, my friend Dick Kiley—the actor—and I were out by the lake and somehow got the idea that we should take turns frightening each other by pretending to be movie monsters. For each quick change, we would run behind a tree and arrange our hair or jackets to suit the role.

At a certain point it occurred to me to take my sweater off, roll it up into a ball, and stick it under my jacket so that I looked like the Hunchback of

Notre Dame. I smeared my hair down into my eyes, rubbed dirt onto my face, and walked out toward Dick, dragging one leg behind me. I looked so horrible, I almost frightened myself! To make the act even more convincing, I made a lot of noise—groaning and roaring.

Dick was saying, "Fantastic! Really looks scary," when right in the middle of my performance three flashlight beams landed on me from out of the darkness. A voice said, "Stop right there, you son-of-a----!" It was the police. Apparently they had heard the noise and were investigating its cause. It took a little fast talking for Dick and me to get out of that one!

It was in the year of our Lord 1939 that my mother, Aunt Margaret, and I went through an experience that not many will ever be privileged to share. We were on hand when the world came to an end.

The occasion was the famous Orson Welles *The War of the Worlds* broadcast. I never told the story of my own response to that broadcast before I first wrote about it in *Mark It and Strike It* and then more recently when I rewrote the story for an Orson Welles tribute. I've seen the reaction of those who were not victimized by Welles to those who were. It's the standard reaction of the level-headed citizen to the crackpot. Nevertheless, millions of otherwise normal Americans were made fearful by the program because it was presented as a newscast.

At the time of the broadcast, I was reading a book in a room on the eighth floor of the Hotel Raleigh, an ancient and run-down hostelry on Chicago's near north side that was our home that year. Feeling in the mood for background music, I turned on our radio, fiddled with the dial until I heard dance music, and returned to my book. After a moment the music was interrupted by a special "flash" from the CBS news department. A scientist had just detected a series of gaseous explosions on the planet Mars.

There soon followed a series of bulletins, each more exciting than its predecessor, revealing that the strange explosions on Mars had caused a downpour of meteors in the area of Princeton, New Jersey. Because the information was presented as a newscast, there was not the slightest reason to question the truth of what was being said. After all, if Dan Rather told you something tonight on his evening broadcast, you would believe it.

I had cast aside my book and was sitting cross-legged by the radio, listening with mounting horror while the network news department brought listeners up-to-the-minute reports on what was transpiring in New Jersey. A special-events man from CBS, who was on the scene near Princeton, reported that one of the Martian meteors appeared to be some sort of spaceship. Bolts and hinges were in evidence.

By this time my mother and Aunt Mag, who had been in an adjoining room playing cards, were huddled around the radio's speaker, wide-eyed.

An army officer made a dignified plea over the radio for calm, but he was interrupted by the network with another report from the scene. Fearful listeners were treated to the benumbing description, by a frightened newsman, of the emergence of strange leathery creatures from the spaceship.

"Good God," my Aunt Mag gasped, her face pale. "What's going on?"

"I don't know," I said. "What do you think we ought to do?"

"There's only one thing *to* do," my mother responded. "We can all go over to church and wait there to see what happens." She was referring to the Holy Name Cathedral, not many blocks from our hotel.

Just then a voice on the radio intoned, "More spaceships have been reported. Observers have seen them over Cleveland, Detroit, and Chicago."

"Jesus, Mary, and Joseph!" Aunt Mag shouted. "We'll be killed right here in this hotel!" She ran into the other room and grabbed her coat. I buttoned my own overcoat, and we hurried out to let other people in on our secret.

The hotel lobby, which we had expected to find in turmoil, was a scene of traditional, lobby-like calm. People were sitting about, smoking cigars, reading newspapers, speaking in subdued tones, or dozing peacefully in thick leather chairs.

It had been our intention to sweep through the lobby and proceed right across Dearborn Street, pausing only in the event that a sudden spaceship attack should force us to take cover, but something about the tranquility around the registration desk presented a challenge we did not feel strong enough to resist. Indeed, we felt it our duty to warn the unfortunate souls who thought all was well that they were about to witness ultimate disaster.

"Is something wrong?" a blasé desk clerk asked quietly, evidently hoping that if anything were amiss he could contain the area of alarm within his immediate vicinity.

"Well," said my aunt with a contemptuous sneer, "it's the end of the *world*, that's all that's wrong!"

The clerk's face was an impenetrable mask, although after a moment, he permitted a suggestion of disdain to appear on it. I started to explain that "on the radio...." Then in some clear, calm corner of my mind I heard something. It was a radio making soft sounds in a corner of the lobby, and the sounds were not the sort a radio should be making at a time of worldwide crisis. The sounds, as a matter of fact, were of a commercial nature. Some other announcer on some other station was extolling the virtues of a brand of tomato soup.

A wave of shock passed through me as I saw things as they really were. Turning to my mother, I began speaking fast, explaining exactly what had happened. For a split second she wavered, hoping, yet fearing, and then for her, too, the ice broke.

Light, followed by painful embarrassment, also dawned on Aunt Mag. Like bewildered sheep we retreated, excruciatingly aware that all heads were turned toward us, that the clerk was smiling at us in a frightfully patronizing way, and that never again as long as we lived would we be able to walk through that Chicago hotel lobby without casting our eyes to the floor.

I knew many lovely people and families in Chicago as a youth. In fact, I not only remember the names of my childhood friends, I can still say them backwards! It sounds like a strange accomplishment, but I went to the trouble to figure them out and have never forgotten them. John O'Rourke was Nhoj Ekruoro; Jack St. Leger was Kcaj Ts. Regel; Robert Petrolli was Trebor Illortep. Other friends included Richard Kiley, Jim Driscoll, and Tommy Monahan. There was Elaine Hill, who was my girlfriend of sorts for a few months. I often visited the Mahoneys and the Glosters, whose father was a fireman.

Today I have the pleasure of visiting Chicago only on rare occasions for performances, but it's a city I greatly enjoy. It's big and exciting. I'm sure everyone living there is aware of its virtues. You merely have to look through the following pages to understand its appeal.

■

THERE IS SOMETHING INEVITABLE ABOUT CHICAGO.

SHERWOOD ANDERSON

From *Sherwood Anderson's Memoirs.* Originally from Ohio, Sherwood Anderson dropped out of high school and followed his brother Karl, a painter, to Chicago. During the next 30 years he produced many masterful works, including *Dark Laughter, The Triumph of the Egg,* and *Winesburg, Ohio.*

(Overleaf, pages 20-21) Chicago Skyline and Lake Michigan. (Above) Chicago Board of Trade Building. Designed by Holabird and Root, the 1930 block-long, art-deco structure houses the world's largest commodities exchange. The figures in relief above the front entrance are by Alvin Meyer, and they hold bundles of wheat and corn, the major commodities traded here. (Facing) "The Pioneers," Michigan Avenue Bridge. Henry Hering's limestone sculpture honors the men and women who settled the American West.

Wrigley Building. Built by Graham, Anderson, Probst, and White in the 1920s, the structure features intricate ornamentation inspired by Renaissance designs. It was commissioned by chewing-gum magnate William Wrigley Jr., who wanted anyone approaching the structure from the south to think that the building was rising from the middle of Michigan Avenue.

Museum of Science and Industry. Built for the 1893 World's Columbian Exposition, the museum served as the fair's fine arts building. It was modeled after classic Greek architecture and decorated with replicas of Greek and Renaissance masterpieces. The exposition commemorated the 400th anniversary of Christopher Columbus's discovery of the Western Hemisphere.

LAY ME ON AN ANVIL, O GOD.

BEAT ME AND HAMMER ME INTO A STEEL SPIKE.

DRIVE ME INTO THE GIRDERS THAT HOLD A SKYSCRAPER TOGETHER.

TAKE RED-HOT RIVETS AND FASTEN ME INTO THE CENTRAL GIRDERS.

LET ME BE THE GREAT NAIL HOLDING A SKYSCRAPER THROUGH

BLUE NIGHTS INTO WHITE STARS.

CARL SANDBURG

From "Prayers of Steel," in *Cornhuskers*. Carl Sandburg was a columnist, editorial writer, and feature
writer for the *Chicago Daily News* from 1918 to 1933. During that time he published *The Chicago Race
Riots*. His other works include *Chicago Poems, Smoke and Steel,* and *Slabs of the Sunbaked West*.

*Madison Plaza. Designed by the architectural firm of Skidmore, Owings & Merrill, the
office complex features a lobby made of white marble.*

Lake Point Tower. At 70 stories the tower was the tallest reinforced concrete building in the world at the time of its completion in 1968. It was designed by John Heinrich and George Schipporeit after a project proposed by Ludwig Mies van der Rohe.

(Overleaf, pages 28-29) Marina City. Bertrand Goldberg, a student of Ludwig Mies van der Rohe, designed the 60-story twin concrete towers in 1964. (Above) Bellman, Ritz-Carlton Hotel, Water Tower Place. (Facing) Detail, Orchestra Hall. Home to the Chicago Symphony Orchestra, the hall also features concerts by the Civic Orchestra of Chicago, as well as other musical attractions.

THE FREE SPIRIT IS THE SPIRIT OF JOY.
IT DELIGHTS TO CREATE IN BEAUTY.

LOUIS SULLIVAN

From *The Autobiography of an Idea*. One of the great leaders
in early modern architectural design was Louis Sullivan. During his partnership with engineer Dankmar Adler in Chicago,
he produced some of his best works, including the Auditorium
Building in 1883 and the Transportation Building for Chicago's
Columbian Exposition of 1893.

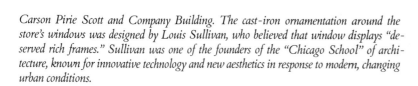

*Carson Pirie Scott and Company Building. The cast-iron ornamentation around the
store's windows was designed by Louis Sullivan, who believed that window displays "de-
served rich frames." Sullivan was one of the founders of the "Chicago School" of architecture, known for innovative technology and new aesthetics in response to modern, changing
urban conditions.*

Chicago School of Ballet.

ANY WORK, GREAT AS HUMAN EXPRESSION,
MUST BE STUDIED IN RELATION TO THE
TIME IN WHICH IT INSISTED UPON ITS
VIRTUES AND GOT ITSELF INTO HUMAN VIEW.

FRANK LLOYD WRIGHT

From *An Autobiography of Frank Lloyd Wright*. Born in Wisconsin in 1869, Frank Lloyd Wright left for Chicago at the age of 18. His first job was as a draftsman for architect Joseph Lyman Silsbee. He later worked for the firm of Adler & Sullivan, where he studied under architectural master Louis Sullivan, who encouraged the development of new approaches to modern architecture.

(Overleaf, pages 34-35) South Lagoon, Lincoln Park. Built with rowing teams in mind, the lagoon's rectangular shape is an ideal practice facility. Crews enter the lagoon through Diversey Harbor. (Overleaf, pages 36-37) Buckingham Fountain. (Above) "Sunday Afternoon on the Island of La Grande Jatte," Art Institute of Chicago. Georges Seurat's painting is one of many internationally acclaimed impressionist masterpieces on display at the institute.

Art Institute of Chicago. In 1893 Edward Kemeys cast the two bronze lions that guard the entrance to the institute. Self taught, Kemeys was the first American sculptor to concentrate on animal subjects, particularly wild beasts.

Chicago Board of Trade.

Skyline. When Father Jacques Marquette and Louis Jolliet of France explored the Chicago area in 1673, they used a short cut to get from the Mississippi River waterways system to the Chicago River. Called "the Portage," this was the swampy marshland on which Chicago was built.

I WAS NEVER QUITE SATISFIED WITH ANYTHING, BUT ALWAYS
LOOKED FORWARD TO DOING SOMETHING BETTER.

GEORGE M. PULLMAN

In 1881 George M. Pullman, inventor of the Pullman sleeping car, built the company town of Pullman,
Illinois, which is now part of the city of Chicago.

*(Above) Train yard. By 1860 Chicago was the center of the largest rail network in the
world. George Pullman established his famous railroad-car factory, the Pullman Palace
Car Company, here in 1867. (Facing) Sears Tower. Even in a high wind, the top of the
1,454-foot Sears Tower never sways more than six inches.*

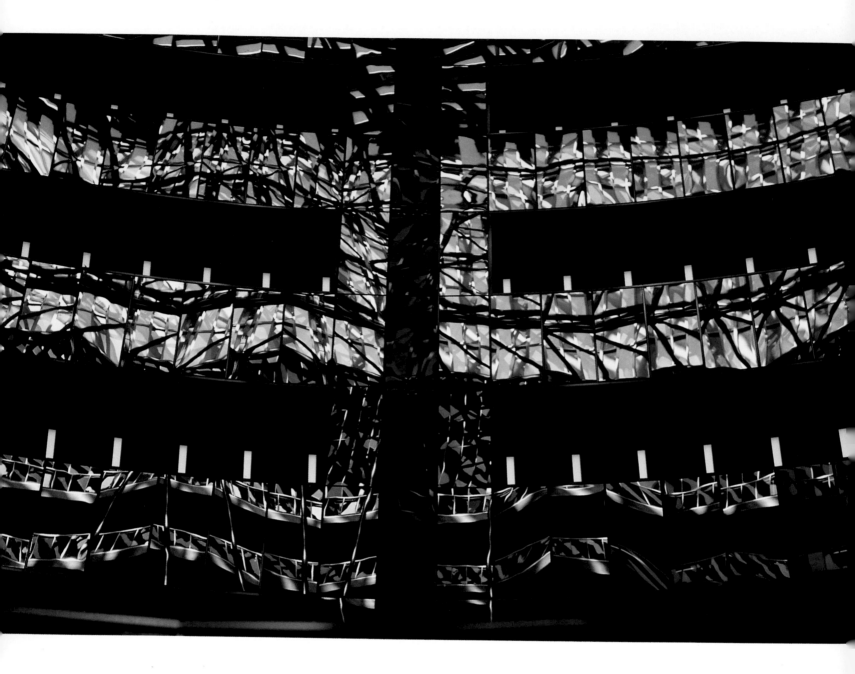

I DO NOT THINK ANY OF US QUITE KNOW HOW MUCH OUR POINT OF VIEW, AND, IN FACT ALL OF OUR TOUCH WITH LIFE, IS INFLUENCED BY OUR IMAGINATION.

SHERWOOD ANDERSON

From "Man and His Imagination" by Sherwood Anderson in *The Intent of the Artist*. Many of Anderson's short stories, novels, and autobiographical works were written in Chicago. They are strongly American and naturalistic. Among his best-known are *The Modern Writer*, *Marching Men*, *A New Testament*, and *Death in the Woods and Other Stories*.

(Above) State of Illinois Center. Architect Helmut Jahn designed the 17-story, glass-and-steel building, which draws 2.5 million visitors yearly. (Facing) "Chicago Picasso," Richard J. Daley Center. The 162-ton corrosive-tensile-steel sculpture was unveiled in 1967. One of the many interpretations of the Cubist work suggests that it resembles a Russian wolfhound that the late Picasso once owned.

First National Bank Plaza.

THE CITY IS BEST SHOWN BY THE WAY IN
WHICH ITS PEOPLE RISE HUMANLY AND WITH
UNDERSTANDING TO ISSUES OF MOMENT.

EDGAR LEE MASTERS

From *The Tale of Chicago*. Edgar Lee Masters was a successful Chicago lawyer as
well as a celebrated author. His widely acclaimed *Spoon River Anthology* is a book
of free-verse "epitaphs" revealing the secret lives of persons buried in a Midwestern
cemetery.

*McCormick Place. Located along the lake front, the metropolitan exposition building was
named for Robert R. McCormick, former owner of* The Chicago Times *and a relative of
Cyrus McCormick, who invented the reaping machine in 1831.*

47

THE MOST IMPRESSIVE FIRST SIGHT OF
THE MIDWEST IS WHEN YOU FLY INTO
CHICAGO AT NIGHT FROM THE EAST,
DESCENDING OVER THE BLACKNESS
OF THE PRAIRIE TO THE...BRILLIANT
RECTANGLES FORMED BY A THOUSAND
SQUARE MILES OF STRAIGHT STREETS
AND BUILDINGS.

GRAHAM HUTTON

From *Midwest at Noon*. Graham Hutton came to the United States
from England in 1937. For eight years he directed the Office of
British Information in Chicago. During that time, Hutton traveled
extensively throughout the Midwest and grew to admire Chicago
and its people greatly.

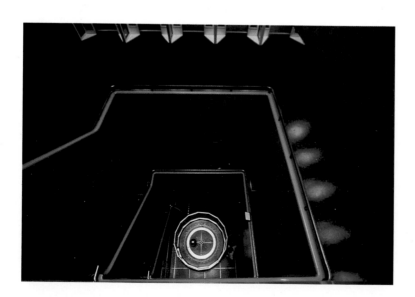

*Museum of Science and Industry. Among other interesting exhibits, the museum houses
an art-science gallery, a U-505 German World War II submarine, a coal mine, and the
National Business Hall of Fame.*

Skyline from Sears Tower. From the observation deck on the 103rd floor of the Sears Tower, one can see the states of Illinois, Indiana, Michigan, and Wisconsin.

(Above) Taxi boat, Chicago River. To prevent the pollution of Lake Michigan, Chicago reversed the flow of the Chicago River and installed a city-wide sewer system. Since the swampy subsoil prevented the sewer pipes from being buried deeply underground, Chicago's streets were raised to cover the pipes. Consequently, the front doors of many homes were blocked, and residents had to build stairs to new doors cut into second-story facades. (Facing) Standard Oil Building.

"Sounding," Standard Oil Building Plaza. Harry Bertoia's unique sculpture features 11 separate units of hard copper-alloy rods, which produce sounds when stirred by the breeze.

"The Four Seasons," the Loop. Russian-born Marc Chagall's five-sided mosaic is 70 feet long and is made of hand-chipped stone and glass fragments from all over the world. Completed in 1974, it depicts six fantasy scenes of Chicago in each of the four seasons.

Tribune Tower. Seeking a design for their new building, the owners of The Chicago Tribune *sponsored an international competition in 1922. Raymond Hood and John Mead Howells won, and their structure was completed in 1925. Eliel Saarinen's second-place entry was revised by Holabird and Roche and became 333 Michigan Avenue, the city's first art-deco skyscraper.*

Chicago Shoreline. A breakwater in the lake separates sailboats from the sweeping gusts of Lake Michigan. Chicago's infamous breezes are said to have originated the "Windy City" nickname.

55

Art Institute of Chicago.

"Ontario," Fountain of the Great Lakes, Art Institute of Chicago. Comprising five female statues by Illinois-native Lorado Taft, the fountain was designed to symbolize each of the Great Lakes. Water flowing from one figure to another in the structure represents the actual course taken by the waters of the lake system.

Triton Fountain, Art Institute of Chicago. Sculptor Carl Milles designed the four half-human, half-fish figures of the fountain to complement the grounds of the Alexander McKinlock Jr. Memorial Court, named by a Chicago philanthropist in honor of his son who was killed in France during World War I.

Tulips, Grant Park. Urbs in Horto, *the motto that adorns Chicago's city seal, means "city in a garden."*

(Overleaf, pages 60-61) Midtown. (Above) "Flamingo," Federal Center. Alexander Calder designed his 50-ton, red-steel sculpture to sit on points and appear weightless. Most famous for his "mobiles," works set in motion by motors or air currents, Calder used the term "stabiles" to define non-moving sculptures such as this one. (Facing) "Man Enters the Cosmos," Max Adler Planetarium. The 13-foot-high bronze sundial was designed by British sculptor Henry Moore to commemorate the planetarium's "Golden Years of Astronomy" from 1930 to 1980. The award-winning planetarium was designed by architect Ernest Grunsfeld Jr.

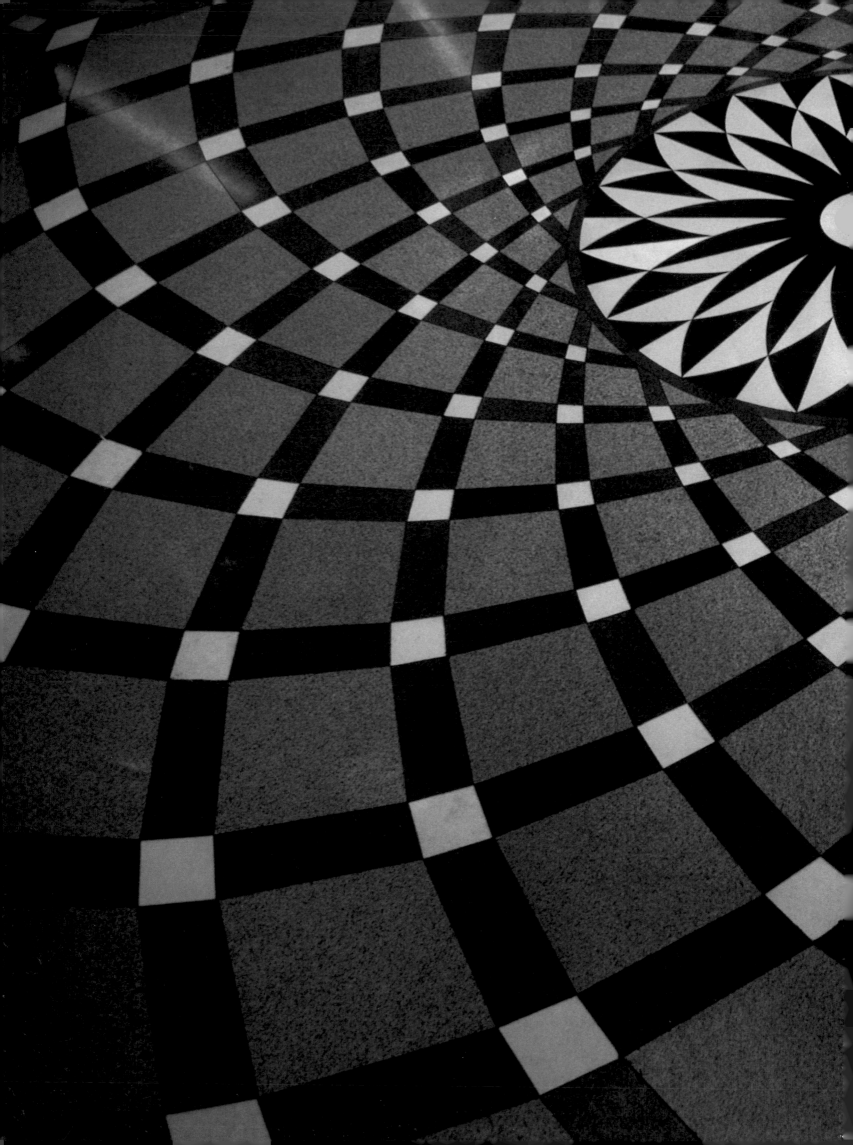

(Overleaf, pages 64-65) State of Illinois Center. The state center soars upward from a marble rosette embedded in the center of a granite floor to the top of a 332-foot atrium. (Above) State of Illinois Center.

St. Patrick's Day Parade. After fleeing Ireland's Great Famine in the 1840s, Irish families became the first large group of immigrants to settle in Chicago. They helped build the burgeoning city and were especially influential in Chicago politics. Each year the Chicago River is dyed green for the Irish holiday.

(Above) Art Institute of Chicago Plaza. (Facing) Baha'i House of Worship. Built in 1933, the Baha'i temple has nine sides and nine entrances. The number nine is a symbol of unity in the Baha'i faith.

(Above and facing) DePaul University. Originally chartered as St. Vincent's College,
DePaul University was granted its own charter in 1907.

THE SECRET OF ALL GREAT UNDERTAKINGS
IS HARD WORK AND SELF-RELIANCE.

GUSTAVUS FRANKLIN SWIFT

From *The University of Chicago Biographical Sketches* by Thomas Wakefield
Goodspeed. Gustavus F. Swift, founder of Swift and Company, revolu-
tionized the meat-packing industry when his firm opened a national mar-
ket for dressed beef shipped in refrigerated railroad cars.

(Above) Pizzeria Due, Wabash Avenue. (Facing) Buckingham Fountain. Kate Buckingham, a wealthy Chicagoan, gave the world's largest decorative fountain to Chicago in 1927 as a memorial to her brother Clarence, a former director of the Chicago Art Institute. At night the three-tiered fountain of pink Georgian marble is lit by 653 colored lamps.

(Above) Lighthouse and pump, Lake Michigan. As the largest fresh-water body in the United States and the sixth largest in the world, Lake Michigan has a 22,400-square-mile surface area. (Facing) Skyline. One hundred years after Marquette and Jolliet explored the area of "Checagou"—the Indian term for wild onion—a trading post was established on the Chicago River. By 1803 the post had been replaced by Fort Dearborn. In 1833 Chicago became a town, and on March 4, 1837, a city.

Gold Coast. The luxurious residential area north of Michigan Avenue boasts elegant
mansions, townhouses, and high-rise condominiums.

C.D. Peacock Jewelry Store. The State Street store is the city's oldest commercial establishment, founded in 1837.

(Overleaf, 78-79) Northwestern University. Located in Evanston, Illinois, the university opened its doors in 1855. Its buildings include the Dearborn Observatory and the Technological Institute. (Above) Northern suburbs. (Facing) Lakefront homes.

(Overleaf, pages 82-83) Mackinac Island Sailboat Race, Lake Michigan. Sponsored by the Chicago Yacht Club each summer, the race finds sailors departing Monroe Harbor for Mackinac Island, about 333 miles away. (Above and facing) Lake Michigan beach.

THIS IS THE URGENCY: LIVE!
AND HAVE YOUR BLOOMING IN THE NOISE OF THE WHIRLWIND.

GWENDOLYN BROOKS

From "The Second Sermon on the Warpland," in *The World of Gwendolyn Brooks*. Born in Topeka and raised in Chicago, Gwendolyn Brooks published her first poem when she was 13 and more than 75 other verses before she was 20. In 1950 she won the Pulitzer Prize for a collection of poems called *Annie Allen*. Her novel *Maud Martha* tells the story of a black girl's childhood in Chicago.

(Above) Community playground. The first game of softball was played indoors at Chicago's Farragut Boat Club in 1887. Invented by George Hancock, softball—known at that time as "diamond ball," "fast ball," and "kitten ball"—was played with broomsticks and boxing gloves. (Facing) Downtown.

(Above) "The Four Seasons," the Loop. (Facing) Belmont Harbor, Lake Michigan.
Mariners who dock at Belmont Harbor are ferried by dinghies to the shore and vice versa.

Frederick C. Robie House, Hyde Park. Now owned by the University of Chicago, the Robie House was built in 1909 by Frank Lloyd Wright, who believed the structure was his best residential design.

THESE CREATIONS OF OURS! I SEE AS WE
LOOK BACK UPON THEM, OR AS WE LOOK
AT THEM AND TRY TO RE-CREATE THEM,
HOW WE OURSELVES BELONG TO THEM.

FRANK LLOYD WRIGHT

From *An Autobiography of Frank Lloyd Wright.* Some of the architect's most
memorable buildings include a series of Prairie-style houses first developed
in Chicago, which culminated in his two residences, Taliesin in Wisconsin
and Taliesin West in Arizona. Taliesin — "Shining Brow" — is the name of a
mythical bard credited with preserving ancient Welsh literature.

*Detail, Frank Lloyd Wright Home and Studio, Oak Park. Born in Richland Center,
Wisconsin, renowned architect Frank Lloyd Wright developed his "Prairie" style—homes
with low horizontal lines and projecting eaves—in the Chicago area.*

"March of Religion," Rockefeller Memorial Chapel, University of Chicago. The 15 life-size religious figures were designed by Ulric Ellerhusen and Lee Lawrie. The chapel bears the name of John D. Rockefeller, whose generous gifts enabled the university to open in 1892.

University of Chicago.

93

University of Chicago. Famous for its research and graduate work, the university houses the Ogden Graduate School of Science, the Institute for the Study of Metals, the Oriental Institute, the Enrico Fermi Institute of Nuclear Studies, and the University of Chicago Press.

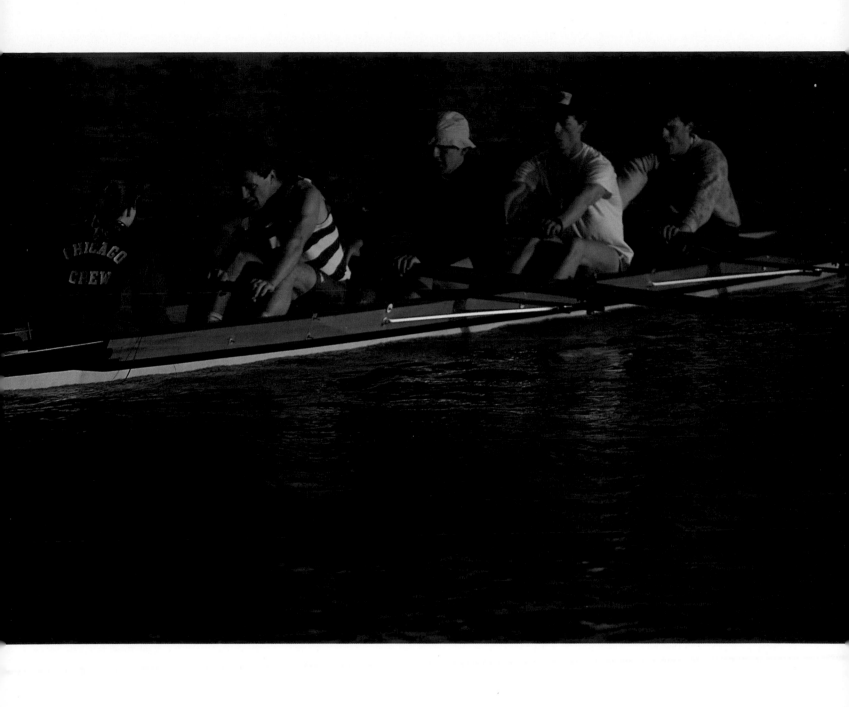

Crew team.

I STOOD AND GAZED AT THE BUSY TRACKS IN THE RAILROAD

YARDS BELOW ME, AT THE LINE OF HIGH WAREHOUSES ALONG

THE RIVER...THE THOUGHT OF MY BRAIN, THE LABOR OF MY BODY,

THE WILL WITHIN ME HAD GONE TO THE MAKING OF THIS WORLD.

ROBERT HERRICK

From *The Memoirs of an American Citizen*. After graduating from Harvard in 1890, American novelist Robert Herrick spent most of his teaching career at the University of Chicago. His realistic novels include *The Common Lot*, *Together*, *The Master of the Inn*, and *One Woman's Life*.

Downtown.

Shipping containers. The opening of the St. Lawrence Seaway in 1959 made Chicago an important international seaport. Iron, steel, and wheat are routinely shipped from Chicago to places around the world.

THE MOST IMPRESSIVE FIRST SIGHT OF THE MIDWEST IS WHEN YOU FLY
INTO CHICAGO AT NIGHT FROM THE EAST, DESCENDING OVER THE
BLACKNESS OF THE PRAIRIE TO THE…BRILLIANT RECTANGLES FORMED
BY A THOUSAND SQUARE MILES OF STRAIGHT STREETS AND BUILDINGS.

GRAHAM HUTTON

From *Midwest at Noon*. Graham Hutton came to the United States from England in 1937. For eight years he directed the Office of British Information in Chicago. During that time, Hutton traveled extensively throughout the Midwest and grew to admire Chicago and its people greatly.

(Overleaf, pages 98-99) United Terminal, O'Hare International Airport. The steel-, aluminum-, and glass-vaulted concourse was designed by Helmut Jahn to provide a prominent architectural gateway to the city. (Overleaf, 100-101) Western suburbs from Sears Tower. (Above) O'Hare International Airport. The hub of the nation's air-transportation system, O'Hare has been called "The World's Busiest Airport." Around 125,000 passengers a day—or 40 million each year—arrive here from all points of the globe.

WHEN I VISIT ANY OTHER GREAT CITY OF THE WORLD, I AM A GUEST.
WHEN I AM IN CHICAGO, I AM AT HOME.

SHERWOOD ANDERSON

From *Sherwood Anderson's Memoirs*. Anderson's unique style of writing had a large impact
on American letters. Ernest Hemingway and William Faulkner, with whom Anderson
shared an apartment in New Orleans, credit him with influencing their style.

Western suburbs.

IN THE WORDS OF CANON BARNETT...THE THINGS
WHICH MAKE MEN ALIKE ARE FINER AND BETTER
THAN THE THINGS THAT KEEP THEM APART.

JANE ADDAMS

From *Twenty Years at Hull House*. Long an admirer of English clergyman and social worker
Samuel Augustus Barnett, who started England's first settlement home, Jane Addams
founded Chicago's Hull House on September 18, 1889. In 1931 she and American educator
Nicholas Murray Butler shared the Nobel Peace Prize for their efforts on behalf of international peace.

*(Above) Northwestern University. (Facing) Jane Addams' Hull House. The original
owner, Charles Hull, left the house in the 1870s, at a time when the neighborhood was
becoming surrounded by factories and tenement houses. Social reformer Jane Addams
later turned the building into a welfare center that lobbied for child labor reform, better
housing, and an increase of parks and playgrounds for Chicago's poor.*

Madison Street Bridge.

Sears Tower and Lake Michigan.

(Above and facing) Buckingham Fountain. Bronze sea monsters, each 20 feet long, encircle the base pool. They represent Illinois, Indiana, Michigan, and Wisconsin—the four states that border Lake Michigan. The sculptures were created by French artist Marcel Loyau. At its greatest diameter, the fountain spans 280 feet. Its central column of water rises 135 feet.

MEN DO NOT EXIST IN FACTS. THEY EXIST IN DREAMS.

SHERWOOD ANDERSON

From *Sherwood Anderson's Memoirs.* Literary historians consider Sherwood Anderson to be a member of the Chicago "Renaissance" writers group, which included novelist/playwright Floyd Dell, poet Carl Sandburg, and author Theodore Dreiser.

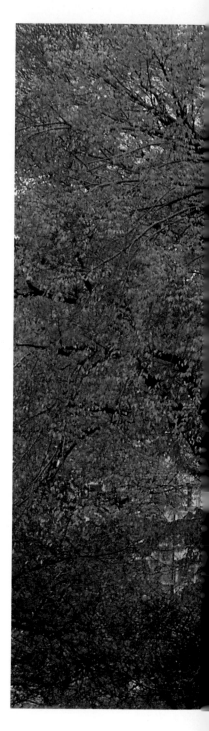

Ballet class.

*Grant Park. The lake-front park contains American sculptor Augustus Saint-Gaudens'
statue of Abraham Lincoln, a yacht basin, and numerous gardens.*

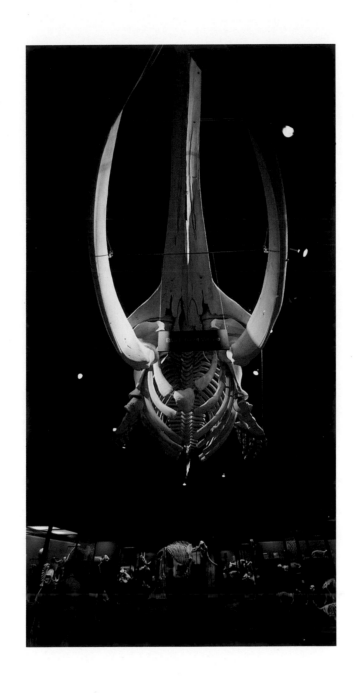

(Above and facing) Field Museum of Natural History. An $8 million bequest in the will of American merchant Marshall Field provided funding for the museum, which houses more than 15 million artifacts and specimens. Like the Museum of Science and Industry, the Field Museum is a legacy from the 1893 Columbian Exposition. It was designed as a permanent home for the collections brought to Chicago for the fair.

THE ORDER OF CHANGE IS LIMITLESS AND PROFOUND.

FRANK LLOYD WRIGHT

From *An Autobiography of Frank Lloyd Wright*. The premiere American architect of his time, Wright felt that people's homes were not independent entities but part of a larger landscape complex. His empathy with Japanese architecture resulted in his commission to design the Imperial Hotel in Tokyo. His engineering triumph survived Japan's 1923 earthquake unscathed.

(Overleaf, pages 114-115) Downtown from Sears Tower. (Above) Associates Building.

John G. Shedd Aquarium. Situated on the lake shore, the white-walled home to the world's largest indoor aquarium displays fresh and saltwater fish, invertebrates, mammals, and reptiles.

(Above) "The Spirit of Music," Theodore Thomas Memorial, Grant Park. Albin Polasek's 15-foot bronze personification of classical music originally stood across from Orchestra Hall, which once housed Theodore Thomas' Chicago Orchestra. (Facing) Grant Park.

THE STREETS ARE CROSSED AND INVADED BY THE METALLIC
STRUCTURE...COMMONLY KNOWN AS THE EL. THIS LOW
STEEL CEILING TRANSFORMS THE AVENUES INTO DARK
TUNNELS; BEAMS THAT ARE SHAKEN BY THE PASSING TRAINS
FILL THE AIR WITH GROANS THAT PENETRATE THE HOUSES:
IT IS A GREAT VOICE LIKE THE VOICE OF NATURE, OR THAT
OF THE WINDS AND THE FORESTS.

SIMONE DE BEAUVOIR

From *America Day by Day*. Born in Paris in 1908, Simone de Beauvoir was a leading French
novelist, essayist, and existentialist writer. She spent some time in Chicago in the 1940s,
staying with her friend Nelson Algren.

Equitable Building.

The "El." Built to connect the city with the grounds of the 1893 Columbian Exposition, Chicago's elevated railway system proved to be such a success that by 1897 additional lines were linked to form "the Loop," a circuit around the central business district.

(Above) Carriage horse and driver. (Facing) Marshall Field's Clock. According to store legend, the first time Marshall Field overheard a salesperson arguing with a customer, he told the employee to "give the lady what she wants!" That phrase became Marshall Field's company motto.

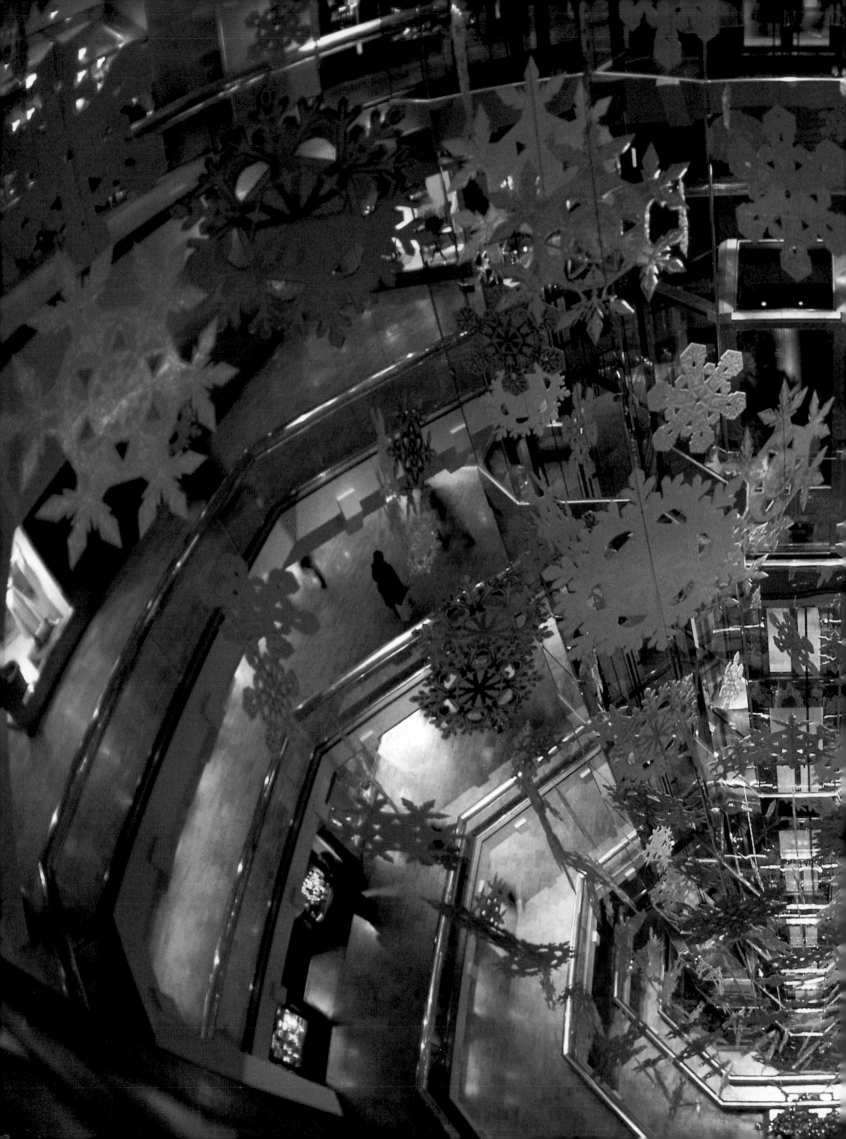

(Overleaf, 124-125) The Magnificent Mile, Michigan Avenue. Located north of the Chicago River, the "Magnificent Mile" is a shopping mecca, featuring one of the highest concentrations of exclusive stores in the world. (Overleaf, 126-127) Water Tower Place. Containing numerous shops, boutiques, restaurants, cinemas, and a hotel, Water Tower Place occupies an entire block along Michigan Avenue. (Above) Poinsettia, Lincoln Park Conservatory. (Facing) Gucci, Michigan Avenue.

MAKE BIG PLANS; AIM HIGH IN HOPE AND WORK, REMEMBERING THAT A NOBLE LOGICAL DIAGRAM ONCE RECORDED WILL NEVER DIE BUT LONG AFTER WE ARE GONE WILL BE A LIVING THING, ASSERTING WITH GROWING INTENSITY.

DANIEL H. BURNHAM

Architect Daniel Burnham founded the Chicago firm Burnham & Root, whose 10-story Montauk Building was the first in the nation to be called a "sky scraper." After his partner's death, Burnham formed D.H. Burnham & Company and was chosen as architectural administrator for the 1893 World's Columbian Exposition. He was a pioneer in city planning.

(Above) Old Chicago Water Tower. Constructed in 1869, the water tower and pumping station are the only public buildings that survived the great Chicago fire of 1871. The legendary inferno was blamed on Patrick and Katherine O'Leary's cow, which allegedly kicked over a kerosene lantern in their barn. The disaster destroyed one-third of the city, but Chicago doubled its population in the following decade. (Facing) Sears Tower. (Overleaf, pages 132-133) Skyline from Adler Planetarium. (Overleaf, pages 134-135) Water Tower Plaza.

AND NEVER ONCE, ON ANY MIDNIGHT WHATSOEVER,

WILL YOU TAKE OFF FROM HERE WITHOUT A PANG.

WITHOUT FOREVER FEELING SOMETHING PRICELESS

IS BEING LEFT BEHIND IN THE FOREST OF FURNISHED

ROOMS, LOST FOREVER DOWN BELOW, BENEATH

THE MILES AND MILES OF LIGHTS AND LIGHTS.

NELSON ALGREN

From *Chicago: City on the Make*. Nelson Algren, a novelist and short-story writer, grew up in Chicago and graduated from the University of Illinois with a degree in journalism. His first critical success was *Never Come Morning*, the story of Poles living on Chicago's West Side. In 1949 he won the National Book Award for his novel, *The Man With the Golden Arm*.

Excerpt from "Chicago" in *Chicago Poems* by Carl Sandburg, copyright ©1916 by Holt, Rinehart and Winston, Inc., renewed 1944 by Carl Sandburg, reprinted by permission of Harcourt Brace Jovanovich, Inc. Excerpt from "Prayers of Steel" in *Cornhuskers* by Carl Sandburg, copyright ©1918 by Holt, Rinehart and Winston, Inc., renewed 1946 by Carl Sandburg, reprinted by permission of Harcourt Brace Jovanovich, Inc. Excerpts from *Memoirs* by Sherwood Anderson, copyright ©1942 by Eleanor Anderson, renewed 1969 by Eleanor Copenhaver Anderson. Reprinted by permission of Harold Ober Associates Inc. Excerpts from *Autobiography of an Idea* by Louis Sullivan, copyright ©1924 & 1956 by Dover Publications. Excerpts from *An Autobiography* by Frank Lloyd Wright, copyright ©The Frank Lloyd Wright Foundation 1932, all rights reserved. Courtesy of the Frank Lloyd Wright Memorial Foundation. Excerpt from *The Intent of the Artist* by Sherwood Anderson, et al, copyright ©1941 by Princeton University Press, renewed by Princeton University Press. Excerpt from *The Tale of Chicago* by Edgar Lee Masters, copyright ©1933 by G.P. Putnam's Sons. Excerpt from *Midwest at Noon* by Graham Hutton, copyright ©1946 by the University of Chicago Press. Excerpt from *The University of Chicago Biographical Sketches* by Thomas Wakefield Goodspeed, copyright ©1922 by the University of Chicago Press. Reprinted with publisher's permission. Excerpt from "The Second Sermon on the Warpland" by Gwendolyn Brooks in *The World of Gwendolyn Brooks*, 1971, and in *Blacks*, copyright ©1987, The David Company. Reprinted by permission of Gwendolyn Brooks. Excerpt from *The Memoirs of an American Citizen* by Robert Herrick, published 1905 by Macmillan. Excerpt from *Twenty Years at Hull House* by Jane Addams, published 1910 by Macmillan. Excerpt from *America Day by Day* by Simone de Beauvoir, copyright ©1952 by Gerald Duckworth and Co., Ltd. Reprinted by permission of Gerald Duckworth. Excerpt from *Chicago: City on the Make* by Nelson Algren, copyright ©1951 by Doubleday and Co., Inc.

The publisher has made a thorough effort to locate all persons having any rights or interests in the material presented in this book and to secure all necessary reprint permissions. If any required acknowledgments have been omitted inadvertently or any rights overlooked, we regret the error and will correct the oversight in future editions of the book.